ABOVE ALL

ABOVE ALL

SUSAN LYNN BAILEY, MD

Copyright © 2024 by Susan Lynn Bailey, MD

All rights reserved. No part of this publication may be reproduced, distributed, or transmitted in any form or by any means, including photocopying, recording, or other electronic or mechanical methods, without the prior written permission of the copyright owner and the publisher, except in the case of brief quotations embodied in critical reviews and certain other noncommercial uses permitted by copyright law. For permission requests, write to the publisher, "Attention: Permissions Coordinator," to the address below.

Studio of Books LLC
5900 Balcones Drive Suite 100
Austin, Texas 78731
www.studioofbooks.org
Hotline: (254) 800-1183

Ordering Information:
Special discounts are available on quantity purchases by corporations, associations, and others. For details, contact the publisher at the address above.

Printed in the United States of America.

ISBN-13:	Softcover	978-1-964148-32-8
	Hardcover	978-1-964148-33-5
	eBook	978-1-964148-34-2

Library of Congress Control Number: 2024908992
ASIN: B0934NBG32

Table of Contents

The Sinful Nature Prevents Obedience 1

The New Covenant Rescue 7

The Conception of Jesus. 8

Mary 13

Joseph 17

Father God Is the Midwife (Psalm 22:9) 19

Immanuel-God Lives His Life With Us 21

Jesus Knows Trouble is Near (Psalm 22:11) 28

The Second Phase of His Mission 43

God Is a Consuming Fire (Hebrews 12:29) 45

I imagine Jesus as the Word, watching the betrayal play out in the garden and agreeing with His Dad that He is the one to set it all straight again ("The crooked will be made straight." Isaiah 40:4, Luke 3:5). We know He was there when it all started because John tells us that "In the beginning, the Word was there with God" (John 1:1).

He must have felt the same way we feel when we look at pain and injustice when we are young and innocent. You know, it happens when we get the first glimpse of injustice or pain. That first notice of the frailty of humanity touches the place of compassion while we are young and feeling quite capable of making a difference. It may come when you notice a deformity in a classmate, an illness or the death of someone you love, or when someone you care about loses a loved one. You experience or see poverty or social injustice. You imagine this never happening again.

I remember that feeling. Do you remember having that feeling of making a difference and sharing it with someone who agrees with you and helps you believe that you can actually make a difference? Well, imagine Jesus, the Creator of all, wanting to right all that is wrong in the world. ("Nothing was made that was not made by Him" John 1:3.)

He felt invincible because He was invincible. He knew without any doubt that whatever He declared would happen in heaven, but He wasn't going to be in heaven. He was going to have to leave heaven to right all of these wrongs. In heaven, clothed in His glory, and crowned with majesty, He had no authority on earth. Only those clothed in flesh have the authority to make a difference on earth.

He knew that He would have to give up His privileged life as the Ancient of Days, the Son of God. He who has known all things from the beginning to the end would be born into the earth and begin as a Spirit clothed in a tiny human body whose intellect would be influenced by the people who nurtured Him. He would be empty of divine wisdom, as all men begin. He would have to grow in wisdom and stature. He would begin His mission to save the world in the body of a tiny human baby who didn't even know how to obtain food or shelter for himself. If this were not His Father's idea, He would relegate this plan to the realm of the ridiculous and foolish. All He had to do was to grow in wisdom and length. Wisdom is defined as the correct use of knowledge; "discerning or judging what is most just, proper and useful, and if it is to be considered as an acquirement, it is the knowledge and use of what is best, most just, most proper, most conducive to prosperity or happiness." Luke's gospel tells us that Jesus did just that. He was filled with wisdom (Luke 2:40, Luke 2:2).

He knows for sure that He can make a difference because He has spoken an entire universe into being. He knows that He has power. He has never known, seen, or heard of anything that He said not coming forth with the breath of His words (Genesis 1:1–Genesis 3).

Why, the only persons, clothed in flesh or naked spirits, that have ever failed to accomplish what they spoke have been those under the influence of evil and disobedience. Those spirits are the ones who followed Lucifer in his first deception. Now Adam has fallen under the deception of the evil tempter (Genesis 2:4–3:24).

Jesus knows that He can never be deceived because He is God (John 1:1) and He knows everything…everything that is pure and good and true and lovely. He does not know the experience of sin, temptation, or separation from His Dad that comes in the package offered by Satan. And above all, His Dad believes in Him.

He will be the Seed of the woman that will attack the seed of Satan at his head. Jesus is there when His Father declares this. His Father' word is final. Everything will happen just as He says (Isaiah 55:11).

He understands that Satan is so cursed that he will only be able to strike at the heel of His feet (Genesis 3:15).

Satan, the enemy of the precious man, will be defeated once and for all. After Satan's defeat, the beloved man will be restored (Romans 8:17; Hebrews 9:12), the man who so irresponsibly gave away the gift of dominating and speaking spiritual things into physical reality (Matthew 28:18). Jesus will be the one to make a difference. He knows that whatever His Father says, happens, every time.

Now that He is on His mission, He has been abandoned by His Father. The human body that His father specially prepared for Him is now wracked with pain and marred with deformity (Hebrews 10:5, Isaiah 52:14). Jesus calls out to his Dad, and He remembers feeling so secure in His decision to come and redeem the cursed earth and all that is within it. He has to use His faith to feel secure now. He has to believe and not doubt that He will glorify the Father and the Father will glorify Him (John 17:11, John 13:31).

Angels, Abraham, David, and all the faithful ones are waiting and watching. The prophets who were reluctant and those who were bold are all waiting for Him to fulfill the Father's promise. They are all waiting for Him to keep His vow. Jesus imagines how He will praise the Father in front of everyone once the earth is restored back to man (Psalm 22:25).

The prophet Isaiah was bold after the hot coals touched his lips (Isaiah 6:6–7). He spoke out. He told the people how the mission would be accomplished (Isaiah 9:6–7). Isaiah told all who would believe what to expect (Isaiah 7:14, Isaiah 9:6–7). He didn't understand a lot of what he spoke about, but nevertheless, he spoke it out.

Jeremiah explained that God the Father would make a new covenant with the man (Jeremiah 31:31–34). In the first covenant, the law showed man what was truly good and what was evil. Man would experience how wonderful life is when blessings and goodness are in effect and how terrible life is when curses and evil are in force (Deuteronomy 11:26–28).

By presenting these two options to man, God was able to allow people to see that obedience and living God's way brought goodness and blessing, and choosing disobedience brought pain and curses (Deuteronomy 28:15–68).

Jesus' mind drifts back to the cause of all of the curses and pain. The betrayal was presented to the woman as a challenge of the father's love and wisdom (Genesis 3:4–5). The man and woman were made in their image, His Dad's, the Spirit's, and His. He sighs as His own words riffle through His mind. "I and the Father are One" (Genesis 1:26, John 10:30).

The man had a mind, an intellect that gave him the ability to make decisions and have a will of his own. The animals are ruled by instinct, but man can reason far beyond the basic instincts of survival to choose when and how to govern himself and the world around him. Choosing between good and evil was the woman's idea (Genesis 3:5–22). The problem was that she was innocent and did not know or understand what was good and what was evil (Genesis 6:11). Only the Father knows what is good all the time.

Jesus endures this present torture because He believes that His Father knows what is good in heaven and on earth. He feels searing hot pain and thinks. "This does not feel good" (Psalm 22). Then He slowly draws in a breath, and as He breathes through the waves of excruciating pain, His flesh is torn from His body. He reflects. Up to this point, His mission has been successful; He has always said only what His Father said and done what His Father does (John 5:19–20). Obedience, imitating His Father was easy…It's easy to trust someone that you know has perfect knowledge and wisdom, especially when you know that person loves you. THIS PART IS NOT EASY! This is not good!

The woman did not believe in the Father's love or wisdom. Eve did not have the voices of prophets to validate the Father's credibility. The woman, not knowing the difference between what was good and what was evil, probably didn't even realize that her choice to disobey the Father was evil. In her mind, she just wanted to be like God and know more. Only, the "more" she would know would be the evil that the Father had been protecting her from.

When Satan approached Eve, he knew that evil is, and was, everything that opposes God the Father because only God the Father is good. Eve didn't realize that what she and many men through the ages would choose as good would sometimes really be evil (Isaiah 5:20, Judges 21:25). Sin was ushered in, and Jesus knows that only He can neutralize the effects that the presence of sin has on mankind. Sin makes a man do what Satan wants him to do. What Satan wanted Eve to do was itself evil, because it was against the Father's wishes. How did this usher sin and all of the curses into the world? When a human being obeys anyone, the person he obeys becomes his master (Romans 6:16). We know this now because it was revealed to Paul, and he wrote it in his letter to the Romans. Satan then became the ruler of the earth because the man and the woman chose to obey Satan instead of God. God had already given dominion of the earth to the man. Once the man became obedient to Satan, he gave up his God-given authority, becoming a servant to Satan. When man decides he can determine what is good, bad things begin to happen.

God the Father is holy and does not take back what He has given (Numbers 23:19, Samuel 15:29). He gave the man dominion over all the earth (Genesis 1:26) and Adam abdicated his authority to Satan. Satan brought evil into the world. God the Almighty has to allow sickness and pestilence and all the evil from the hearts of men to happen because man chose to become acquainted with evil. The woman was not satisfied with the goodness of God; she wanted her eyes open to evil (Genesis 3:5-6).

Once Adam ate from the Tree of Knowledge of Good and Evil, he became aware of evil (Genesis 3:22). God said that man now knew good and evil. God did not say that man knew the difference between good and evil or could determine which was good and which was evil. Before he ate that fruit, the man had never had contact with evil.

The vegetation now had thorns. Pestilence came into the earth to kill and destroy man. Everything that Jesus created well and good now had an evil component that could either kill or destroy man. This is what Satan willed, and as he became the god of this age, any and everything that could destroy and kill the man came to be common in the man's world (John 10:10).

Satan's mission was to steal what had been given to man, kill and destroy the man. He began to influence man to be selfish and think of himself because now, the man had to provide for himself (John 10:10, 1 John 3:8, Genesis 6:11). His relationship and trust in Father God further deteriorated as Satan told men lies about God. Satan whispered lies among men, and they became angry with one another (John 8:44). Jesus sighs again as He remembers man's degeneration from the glorious creature He created. When Adam was created, he was exactly like the Godhead; he was not acquainted with wickedness, he was not ruled by instinct, but his passion was governed by intellect and reason. There was only wisdom in Adam's thoughts. He could only think of goodness and loveliness and truth (Genesis 1:26). He knew nothing else at all. It is evident that men became less like God and more like the animals. Instinct and self-preservation began to rule his passion. Emotional outbursts began to replace reasoning, and he no longer restrained himself. Adam did not wait to hear advice from the Father but was stirred by Satan's lies, and Satan ruled over him. He used the emotion and passion of the moment to propagate sin. Men decided what was right in their own eyes to make provision from the cursed earth (Judges 21:25). Cain murdered his brother because he envied God's approval of his brother's sacrifice. Cain knew that killing his brother was evil, but he was driven by the passion of his rejection. Afterward, Cain knew in his heart that he should be killed. He begged the Father for protection (Genesis 4:1–16).

Then and many times since, the man was honored and protected by Father God even though the man was guilty of sin. He was not forsaken or disappointed. Jesus cries out to His Father in utter anguish, "Why have you forsaken me?" (Psalm 22) But He knows the answer… and He trusts. Jesus has to believe that He is the Holy One who will not see corruption and that He will be delivered from hell (Psalm 16:10).

Father God's love for the beloved man remains steadfast. Whatever Father said was and is right and good and best for the man. He protected Cain. Father would not allow Abel's murder to be avenged by other men. Thus He averted Satan's plan for the first war (Genesis 4:16).

Jesus' resolve is made stronger, remembering His Father's desire to have a relationship with the man from the very beginning. He recalls His Dad trying to explain to Cain that his sacrifice wasn't acceptable because he didn't do what Father told him to do. But if he did, his sacrifice would be accepted, just as Abel's was (Genesis 4:7). The Father remains the same then and now; if we obey, we will be blessed. Jesus had to trust that at the end of this agonizing pain, He too would be blessed as the rightful ruler over the earth and the kingdom is restored on earth as it is in heaven (Matthew 28:18, Colossians 2:14–15).

The kingdom is restored on earth as it is in heaven (Matthew 28:18, Colossians 2:14–15). As men began to multiply, the influence of the demons increased. The reasoning of men became even more corrupt. Now, men began to reason that the Father sanctioned murder because He showed mercy to Cain (Genesis 4:23–24).

God is only good and only good can be associated with Him. Once the beloved chooses evil, should he be lost to his Creator forever—like Satan? Satan can never go back. There is no provision for him. But because of God's mercy and love for man, the Father made provisions. He injected grace into the relationship between Himself and man.

How brilliantly The Father averted the plans of Satan to destroy man by having sin separate him from the Godhead.

First, Father kept man from being stuck in the perpetual state of evil forever. He did not allow man to eat from the Tree of Life (Genesis 3:22). No choice there, it was guarded by the Lord's warriors. If the man had eaten from the Tree of Life, he would have lived forever in the cursed state once he chose evil. All the evil people would still be living today inflicting pain perpetually; every horrible pest and pain would also be perpetual. Jesus ponders this as His joints are inflamed, swollen, and twisted upon one another, and He experiences wracking pain in every one of them. Mercy will allow His death, and this pain will end; but then, hell's torment will begin. He understands that He can't die until the Father is satisfied that all of the insufferable devastation known to mankind has ravished Him. Then the first part of the mission will be finished. The man's health would be restored. If God had not allowed animal and grain sacrifices, once The Father said he man sinned, goodness would have been removed because there would be no provision for communion and reconciliation with God and His goodness. Goodness only comes from God.

These two provisions by God were the shadows of the "good things" to come, referenced in Hebrews 10:1. Since Jesus is God, He sees all of the time at once (John 1:1). He had knowledge of scriptures before they were written. Therefore, through the centuries, He looked forward to becoming the permanent sacrifice that would allow man to forever be the recipient of blessing and the goodness of God. Just as it was when Adam was first created! Jesus Himself only received, experienced, and thought about goodness and blessing because, in the Kingdom of Heaven, there is nothing else.

Once He sacrificed Himself, Jesus knew for certain that man would no longer be held to the old covenant. The old covenant would become obsolete, just as the Father planned it. One perfect man would keep every command, and it would count for all mankind. Just the way that Adam's rebellion counted for all mankind (Romans 5:12-19, Hebrew 8:13).

Once again, it would be as it was in the garden before the deception. The man would only have to believe in the Father's love for him. The man would only have to believe that Jesus sacrificed Himself in the place of the animals, and the Sacrifice would be eternally accepted for the payment of sins and restoration of health and provision. The man would have to trust the Father's Word (1 Timothy 4:10, Romans 10:9– 10, John 20:31, Mark 11:24, Matthew 21:22).

Hebrews tells us that the first covenant sacrifice rituals were shadows of what was to come (Hebrews 10:1). A shadow is an outline. It has the resemblance of the real object, but no real substance. That is why the rituals had to be done over and over.

A sacrifice of some sort had to be offered to God from the very beginning—even before the law was given. We see the first two siblings offering a sacrifice to God in Genesis (Genesis 4:4–5). This sacrifice was essential to cover the sin that was now a part of man's nature. The sacrifice was essential for fellowship between a Holy God and a man who had chosen to defile himself with a satanic alliance. Understanding this intellectually is one thing, living through this excruciating pain is quite another.

Secondly, by allowing man to use animal sacrifices to absorb man's sin, Father God provided a way to temporarily allow His goodness and blessing to flow to Adam and his off spring, despite man's evil choices. In this way, life on earth was worth living. Jesus' love and admiration for His Father was the driving force, enthralling Him to participate in the plan to keep the man's fellowship. How much His father loved the man and enjoyed the man's love for Him. Often, the Father sang songs over the man, and the man was given voice and melody to sing back to Him (Zephaniah 3:17). Jesus saw the love between His Father and the man. Watching them made His own spirit lift and sing. Jesus couldn't bear the thought of His Father losing the relationship between Himself and man to Satan's hellfire. He witnessed an unconditional love that He knew so well. It is the same love that He feels from His Dad. Nope, above all, He can't let His Father lose that relationship.

The continuation of that fellowship would not have been possible without those yearly sacrifices. The Father is Holy. He cannot interface with sin without consuming it in fire. The burnt offerings were consumed in man's place, allowing the species of man to survive until Jesus Himself could become that Lamb sacrificed as a burnt offering. Jesus knew He would spend time in hell's fire, but He also knew that after the third day,

He would emerge victorious. Though He was the sacrifice that would pass through hell, Jesus Himself could not and would not be consumed because in Him, there was no sin. He is and was the Holy One. He knew that He would be delivered although He had to become sin, taking it into His mortal body (2 Corinthians 5:21, Psalm 16:10).

When Isaiah said, "This new covenant will be like the one given to Noah," it is likely that the analogy was missed. Did you miss it? The story of Noah and the ark has so many things in it to consider, I wonder how many people miss this significant reference to the covenant God made. The covenant that God made with Noah was that He would never send water over the earth and destroy it again. This covenant was unconditional.

No matter how men behaved, no matter how wicked the humans became, He would not destroy them with a flood (Genesis 8:21). His Father swore that once this new covenant went into effect, the man would be reconciled back to Himself without conditions. There would be nothing that man had to do to meet the conditions to be blessed. Just as the promise to Noah was not dependent on man's behavior, this covenant wouldn't depend on man's behavior either. Man would be reconciled back to Him. Father God would never be angry or rebuke the man ever again (Isaiah 54:9). He says that this covenant is a covenant of peace, and it will never be removed. This is what the angels proclaimed when He was born into the earth (Luke 2:14).

"Peace and goodwill toward all men." There would be peace restored between Father and His beloved creation. His loving kindness and mercy will always be with the beloved man. His Father said, "Even if the mountains and hills are removed, I will have mercy on the man" (Isaiah 54:10). Good news! A new covenant would be made between God and man!

In elaborate poetic eloquence, Isaiah also gives the graphic details of how the plan will be executed. As Jesus contemplates the words of the prophet the reality of the price He will pay to install the covenant weighs heavily on Jesus' heart. He does not dwell on Isaiah's prophesies, though. Above all, He thinks about the joy that will be realized once His mission is accomplished and man is again reconciled to his Creator, his Father, his God. (Isaiah 7:14, Isaiah 49:5–8) Of course, I am referring to the seed of Adam because Jesus is not a created being, He was the only 'begotten' Son. (John 3:16)

The Sinful Nature Prevents Obedience

Jesus knew that the old covenant would be replaced by a new one (Hebrews 8:7–13). He Himself would satisfy the demands of the old covenant. The righteousness of God would be revealed to all men and bestowed on all men as a gift (Romans 3:21–26). Christ completely satisfied the just demands of the Holy Father for judgment on sin by His death at Calvary (Hebrews 7:26–28, 1 John 4:10). The old covenant was the covenant of doing good and therefore receiving good (Deuteronomy 28:1–68). Now, a new covenant would take effect. He, Jesus, would be the representative of all men. The representative had to be a man. No Spirit person had the right to participate in the first covenant. The first covenant was made between God and man, and it had to be reckoned between God and Man. Jesus would become a spirit clothed in flesh just like man.

He would be a replica of the man. He would be the God-man. He would live in the body of a man that was prepared by God Almighty (Hebrews 10:5). He would be the first man born with a righteous, sinless spirit inside of Him, because He was—and is—God (John 1:1). We, on the other hand, pass from death to life when we believe the good news. Jesus passed from life to death and then to life again.

Adam was created, and the spirit of God gave him life, but Jesus would be begotten. God cannot and could not be created. He is and always was (Psalm 2:7, John 1:1–2, John 3:16). He would be the example of what a man can do and be if God lived inside of that man. Once the man ate the forbidden fruit, his spirit became dead to his creator. He was now ruled and influenced by the part of him that could be directed by

Satan (John 8:44). He could not overcome the temptations that caused him to choose according to his now corrupt desires. Those desires were fueled by selfishness—what seemed to gratify each man's own desires (Judges 21:25, James 1:14–15).

Sometimes his desire was good, and sometimes his desire was evil. The law was given to the Israelites to show mankind what was good and what was evil by Father's standards. The law has always existed because Father God has always known what is good and what is evil (Mark 10:18).

The plan to reconcile man back to his original state, which would allow him to receive only good from God, was conceived before the foundations of the earth were laid (Ephesians 1:4). The reconciliation had nothing to do with man's obedience to the law. In their infinite wisdom, God the Father, God the Son, and God the Holy Spirit knew that man could not choose good over evil at all times because Satan and his demons were abiding with man. The plan never included man's effort. Men's effort to live godly lives was fruitless for the most part because they were no match for the enticements of Satan. Mankind was given the law as a standard thereby which one could prosper and embark on a better life. The law was never to be obeyed to gain God's love or the gift of immortality, living in paradise or intimacy with the Almighty creator of the universe. The Father has always loved man unconditionally. All of the prior generations before the law existed had no law to follow, yet they received favor, provision, and health from Father by grace. Even before the foolish Israelites entered into the covenant, they had already demonstrated their inability to obey and keep rules (Exodus 16:28).

Jesus was astounded by their lack of insight and poor memory. This is a good example of their disobedient nature: It happened shortly after the Jewish nation was brought safely across the Red Sea. They were given a test to see if they would obey Father God (Exodus 16:14–28). The test went like this: Jesus dropped bread from heaven, and Moses told each man to only gather from the ground, as much as their family could eat each day. He told them not to gather up any to store for later but to trust the Father to have it fall from heaven fresh everyday day (rule number 1).

He told them to gather twice as much bread on the sixth day so that there would be enough left over to eat on the seventh day. If they gathered more than one day's worth on any other day, the bread would spoil. But on the sixth day, the bread would keep overnight and be good to eat on the seventh day (rule number 2).

They couldn't even trust and obey for twenty-four hours of bread. Why did they dare to have their means of blessing be dependent on whether or not they obeyed? Didn't they see they were already cursed? If they had to be obedient to get the manna from heaven, they would have starved. For the first day, some of them gathered more than they were told to gather, and it produced worms (Exodus 16:27). But Dad was faithful, as always. He sent more manna the next day. Now, with good intentions, they shouted, "Give me the rules, and I will do as you say and then we will be your special people."

Well, if the law had already gone into effect, some of them would have been dead the sixth day the manna fell because on the sixth day, some of them tried to store it up and some went out to look for it on the Sabbath. Clearly, these people did not trust His Dad and were not going to obey Him. I imagine the demons must have enticed them to disobey by causing them to doubt God's promise to provide, saying, "You'd better make sure you have some of this manna for hard times. How"How can you be sure God will keep sending it? After all, you did

"How can you be sure God will keep sending it? After all, you did have to go without bread for a time. It could happen again." The evil ones caused men to impede the faith they needed to obey. How sad the three persons of the Godhead were to watch these tiny, helpless human beings running around, storing up the manna as if Dad would not be faithful to keep His word. They disobeyed because they didn't trust God, and that was proof that Satan was still able to influence man. It was proof that given a choice, the man would think he knew how to take care of himself better than Dad did.

As Jesus waited for the appointed time to come to earth, He knew there was no other way but that He should come to earth as a man and feel what He felt He had to hear for Himself the temptations of the evil spirits. It was mind-boggling to Jesus that even when the men sought to do the right thing, they couldn't understand that the right thing was to trust Father God, no matter what. So, as a spirit without flesh, Jesus, the Word, watched, helpless and unable to interfere as men shouted, "We will do everything God says to do. Pitiful!" He thought.

God had provided everything for the man since he had left Egypt. He had not passed the tests of obedience concerning God's provision of manna "How on earth did man think he would keep rules of the law for righteousness sake?" When Father God said, "If you will listen to Me and obey My covenant, you will be My special treasures," they should have said, "We know we cannot obey, and we don't listen. Thank you for bringing us to yourself and 'making' us a holy nation. We'll keep what we have, Your Grace." They had been rescued, held close, and *made* holy by no will of their own. Right before Father mentioned the covenant, He reminded them that He had done everything for them and caused them to triumph over the Egyptians just because *He had already chosen them* over all peoples of the earth Satan could see the whole thing unfolding before his eyes. He couldn't have planned it better himself, he thought. He would use the man's own declaration to God to defeat him and cut the man off from God. Satan would finally be able to kill off all of mankind, and when he went to hell, the precious man's spirit would be right there with him in the eternal fire being tortured as he will be tortured for all eternity. Satan knows that even when the body dies, man's spirit lives on forever. (Matthew 25:41) Satan was well aware that God had to be faithful to His word. Mankind would be destroyed by his own mouth and God's faithfulness to the integrity of His word (Numbers 23:19, Psalm 89:34). That day, the demons were drunk with delight of the anticipated victory. "Strike my head," indeed! Satan thought, *"There won't be a man left alive to strike anything on me!"*

Many, many times, man would fall into disobedience trying to help God out. We are still doing it. How many times have you fallen into disobedience helping God provide for you or fulfill your destiny when His word said that He would provide all your needs? You know that feeling of confidence that comes over you. It's different from the feeling that you can do it because you know that God is with you. This is a different confidence. This is a confidence in what you can accomplish. There is a sense of urgency to get what you want. There is rarely a seeking of the Lord's view. In fact, most often, we don't hear His voice at all. The object or method may be absolutely against the way God's word tells us we are to behave. You're familiar with "A man's (or woman's) gotta do what a man's gotta do" and of course you're doing it your way, only to find that God's way was best and the desired object brought more sorrow than happiness. This is what we can expect whenever we do not follow God's directives, done His way.

When God made Adam, I don't believe that man's mind was originally to accommodate evil. Adam was made in God's image. God is only good, and Adam's mind was programmed to deal with truth, love, and honesty. I don't believe we were ever meant to interact with evil. Therefore, our hearts and minds are not equipped to discern evil, and we are easily deceived. I believe that in his perfect sinless state, when he was created by Jesus, Adam did not have an innate ability to discern evil and deceit. Adam was created in a perfect place. He interacted with his divine family and his wife. There was absolutely no reason for mankind to discern evil and deceit. He could trust whatever he saw and heard to be the unadulterated truth.

Without the Spirit of God's influence, it is difficult for us to discern evil. That is why deception of any kind is always the most successful weapon that Satan has because we are not programmed to see the circumstances or the person for the evil it is. We are programmed to trust. The shrewdest man can be brought down by the betrayal of someone he trusts or ultimately by confidence in his own intellect and the deceit of faith in his own craftiness. Satan deceives us, and he and his demons become the cheering squad for his team that eggs us on. We need the Spirit of God to guide and protect us from the evil that seeks to destroy us. If any man asks God for wisdom, He will give it to him (James 1:5).

Here was the beloved man, once again endeavoring to be the master of his fate. He thought he could choose good over evil and make himself God's treasure by making the correct choices. Hadn't God already made them the most blessed people on the earth as Abraham's descendants? What did Abram do to acquire his blessing? Why hadn't they remembered how well was Abraham treated?

Abraham certainly did not do "everything God told him to do." Despite Abraham's disobedience, he remained God's special friend (Isaiah

41:8, James 2:23). Father God treasured Abraham because Abraham believed that *God would be faithful* to and do what He said He would do. Why they decided that now, they could earn a special place in God's heart by being obedient, was a mystery.

The covenant was full of rules. The covenant was not just the Ten Commandments. It covered everything from personal hygiene and clothing to civil rules and worship. They are listed through several Old Testament books, including Exodus, Leviticus, and Deuteronomy. Mankind has been breaking these rules down through the ages. Most infractions are because mankind has refused to trust God to take care of us. In an effort to preserve our lives, we cheat, we lie. The little white lies are still lies; we deceive with "little" half-truths. All these are reasons enough for God to turn His back. And He did.

The New Covenant Rescue

God turned His back on His own son because of the seemingly "little infringements of the law." Jesus not only took punishment for the "big awful sins," but He was also punished for the ones that seem small to us. Jesus understood that breaking any part of the law caused curses to come on that person. The little white lie sends the lawbreaker straight to hell as sure as murder does (Deuteronomy 28:1, James 2:10).

Jesus recalls the day the Israelites made that declaration and all over again, His heart becomes a heavy weight of sorrow. Their thoughtless, emotionally charged declaration confirmed what He knew. His Spirit had to be clothed inside of a body just like the man's. He had to show man how to fight against the deceptions of Satan because Satan had seduced man.

Satan's demons chanted, "You can do it!", cheering the man on. Man's ego was puffed up with pride, confident they could overcome his deceptions and seductions and earn God's blessings of health, provision, and relationship through obedience. Satan knew better. He was ecstatic! He has an amazing memory. Jesus marvels at the way His Father God makes good His promise to His earthly forefather, David. Jesus understands that He is the Son of God and the Son of man (John 5:26–27). Thus He has authority to interact with Satan spiritually on earth.

The Conception of Jesus

As a physician and a scientist, I don't know why the word fertilization is used in reference to human conception. This physician will never use the term again in reference to conception! Fertilizer is not added to a woman to produce a child. The seed of a woman and the seed of a man has everything in it that will become the child of their union. It is called the genetic code. Advances in modern technology have allowed our generation to see the DNA that we call genetic code, but that is not when the genetic code came into existence. Thus, Cain was made from the genetic code of Adam combined with the genetic code of Eve. Jesus was made from the union of the seed of a woman and the seed of God which is the Word of God. The seed of the Woman and the seed of God had to come together to make flesh and holiness.

The God of the universe begot His son using His divine DNA and DNA from the seed of Mary. It is a scientific fact that the blood of a child comes from his father. Adam's seed contained his genetic code for the blood of his offspring, and God's genetic code contained the DNA to form the Holy blood of Jesus. The Bible tells us that the life of the flesh is in the blood (Leviticus 17:11). Jesus was flesh and He had blood. Since Jesus was begotten by God, His blood was pure, holy, and divine. It was not from a man who inherited the genetic code of Adam. (The life is in the blood (Leviticus 17:110)

God says that He does not change. When He made the man, He said it was good and He rested. Adam and Eve were created full-grown with the seed to reproduce after their own kind. The human seed is ovum (female) and sperm(male). This disproves evolution. Girl apes and boy apes make baby apes. They do not have the genetic code to make a human. At conception, the seed of a man and the seed of a woman unite and a marvelous multiplication occurs forming a zygote. The zygote is transformed into an embryo forming organs by magnificent movements that are "knitted" together just as Psalm 139 says. I believe that man is body soul and spirit because Paul speaks of us that way in 1 Thessalonians.

Admittedly, the genetic code for our spirits and souls is not seen by our scientific technology, but it is present, nevertheless. Spirit is not discernible by flesh and who can see a person's mind, emotions, and intellect that make up his or her soul? The genetic code of the spirit of every man has been inherited from Adam and it is a dead spirit (Ephesians 2:1–3). (1 Corinthians 15:21–22) The Spirit of Jesus in us makes us spiritually alive (Romans 8:10). Adam's physical body did not die immediately when He disobeyed Father God and ate from the tree, but at that very moment, he died spiritually. God meant what He said. "…but of The Tree of Knowledge of good and evil you shall not eat, for in the day that you eat of it you shall surely die." for me to understand that man is knitted in the mother's uterus.

I am a knitter and it is easy for me to understand that man is knitted in the mother's uterus. DNA which determines the embryo's evolution into a fetus as tissue moves to unite forming organs row upon row. Think of it this way. When a garment is made, the knitter follows a pattern using the cords of yarn to form stitches that come together in such a way to form the garment. A ball of yarn is made up of cords. The cords are made of strands, and the strands are made up of fiber. Let's suppose that the pattern for the garment and the intelligence to perform the task were contained inside each fiber of each cord of yarn. If the intelligence and pattern or blueprint needed to form the garment into a particular sweater is contained in the strands of yarn, that strand would represent DNA. Whereas the knitter provides the intellect to follow the pattern to perform stitches that become a particular sweater, the human cells represented by the strands of yarn have the innate intelligence to knit themselves together in order to end up as a child. A ball of yarn is made up of cords. The cords are made up of strands of fiber. The strands of fiber represent the DNA of the spirit, soul, and body of the child. God did not change the manner in which a man is formed.

He set everything up in the beginning and He has not violated His Word that said it is good. Jesus, being a man, was knitted together in Mary's uterus. His "yarn" was made up of both human and divine strands.

If you can understand that God does not violate His word once He has spoken it, you can understand why He does not stop the wicked from performing horrible deeds and He does not prevent the weather from being destructive. He didn't come down to the Garden and stand between Eve and the serpent and He didn't put a high fence around The Tree of Knowledge of Good and Evil. Why? It is because we are made in His image, that's why. God is not restrained. He has the responsibility to make choices and He wanted His beloved man to make the choice to trust Him and obey Him… He still does today. "Without faith, it is impossible to please Him" (Hebrews 11:6).

He gave man dominion over the earth and He gave man the ability to govern his actions by his own will. Jesus operated perfectly with a perfect will. His will was born from a perfect and Holy Spirit. His Spirit carried the genetic code of a perfect God and it was alive when it was knitted to His flesh. He was able to influence the weather, wasn't he? (Matthew 8:24–27, Mark 4:41) If He had not been a man, He would not have had the authority to change the weather, because God gave that authority to man (Genesis 1:28). He will not take it back. He does say that we as spiritually alive humans can move mountains and perform even greater feats with the weather than Jesus did (John 14: 12–14). We must also believe that we can (Mark 11:24). The extent of the manifestation of what we obtain is dependent on the power that works in us, not the power that is in Jesus (Ephesians 3:20).

I have personally controlled weather and animals by speaking and believing in what I spoke. Many others have the same testimony…You can do it too. The purpose of the knitting analogy is to explain Christ's divine and human nature combining to bring about immaculate conception. I am explaining that the words and prophesies proclaiming that Jesus would be born of a virgin, spoken through the years of man's existence functioned as "seed" to bring about the manifestation of an immortal and eternal being who was always called "the Word" and who is human as well. Remember God's Word is Spirit and Life (John 6:63). Thus the Word became flesh. Leviticus 17:11 states that the life of a living being is in its blood. When I was in medical school studying the embryo and fetus and the hematogenesis facts (How blood is made), I learned that the blood of the child comes from the father. I never forgot that. It sounded like a question that might be on the National Boards. Later, when I began to read my bible and hear songs about the precious blood of Jesus, I was blown away by God's ingenuity. He took care of every detail needed to bring about a divine human and hid it from Satan. It was hidden from us too but He has unfolded the mysteries to be shared with those who love Him. (Mark 4:11, Ephesians 3:5, Job 12:22).

It is a scientific fact that the blood of a child comes entirely from the father. The coming together of the prophetic Word of God (which is seed) Look at Luke 8:5–15 and Mary's "seed" produced a man who is 100% human, yet, 100% God. When God speaks, His words bring forth the manifestation of the words spoken. This is how He made everything: He spoke, using His words as 'seed.' Then He said that every living thing would have the seed in themselves to reproduce. Everything initially came from God's spoken words. His words produced as seed does

In order to fulfill the prophecy given regarding the serpent and Eve, the seed of a woman had to be used. In order for Jesus to be God's son, the seed of God (His words) had to join with Mary's human seed, in order for Jesus to have a body. Thus Jesus was begotten and not created. I also want to emphasize that Mary remained a virgin, but a baby grew in her womb in the same fashion as any other baby. In order for the prophecy to be fulfilled regarding the serpent and Eve, the seed of a woman had to be used. His Words had to join with Mary's human seed. There was no other way for Jesus to have a body made of human flesh. God has not changed the method of reproducing humans. If He did, He would violate His word that says everything living has a seed in it and will reproduce after its own kind.

This is the conception of Jesus which makes sense medically and spiritually to be true to the Word of God as stated in the scriptures above that I have listed. Mary certainly was a virgin in the same fashion as any other baby. Mary certainly was a virgin in the sense that no man penetrated her vagina but Jesus did grow in her uterus. I am explaining that Jesus was a flesh and blood man. He was also Holy and God, Since it is a scientific fact that the blood of a human child comes from its father.

Thus the blood of Jesus is Divine. Hopefully you can now understand how the blood of Jesus is Holy, because it is God's blood and not human. That Hes is 100% human and 100% God is the reason He was able to defeat Satan and obtain our legal rigths to dominion over the earth again. The first covenant had to be fulfilled by a man without sin. The battle against Satan had to be fought by a man because the first covenant was made between God and men. If Jesus had been only divine, He would not have been the son of man and thereforeHe would have no authority on earth to defeat Satan (John 5:27).

Mary

For centuries, the prophets have been instructed to communicate to the descendants of Abraham that when Jesus comes to set things right, He will be raised in the home of Jewish parents. King David, who reigned over the chosen ones, was given the promise. A virgin from the king's lineage had to agree to carry the Messiah in her body. Although Father God is all-powerful, He never violates the will of others. He simply asks that we carry out His plan; we can agree to join Him or just say no. Jesus remembers Mary's confusion as He watched from heaven.

Mary asked, "How am I going to have a child? I've never been with a man." He smiles down at her now, weeping on the ground below the cross. That day with Gabriel, she had forgotten the words spoken in the garden by His Father declaring that Seed would be from a woman, not a man (Genesis 3:15). In that way, the manifestation of His body would be possible without the Seed of a human man (Isaiah 7:14).

Jesus would be both God and man. He would be the seed of Mary, human, and the seed of God in the form of the Word of God spoken into Mary's womb by the prophets in the fullness of time. Equally so, Jesus would be a product of conception as every human child is. The conception would be powered by the Holy Spirit (Luke 1:35, Matthew 1:18). In order to have a human body and accomplish His mission on earth, Jesus was born of a woman. This is why Paul says in his epistle to the Hebrew, Jesus being God, is not ashamed to refer to us as His brothers (Hebrews 2:11).

As He watched from heaven, He knew, "she does not yet understand that My Dad prepared a body for me, a human body that will be sacrificed in the place of the animal offerings." She knows that her family and everyone in the Jewish lineage have made animal sacrifices to the Lord year after year. She understands that these sacrifices are made to prevent the penalty of death. That death would include separation from the kingdom of God and all that is good, not just the cessation of life in the body. The animal sacrifices take the penalty of sin and allow God's blessing upon her and her family. Without the animals taking the sin into themselves, the people would be cursed.

Mary knows that the sacrifices only appease God for one year at a time (Hebrews 10:1–7). Mary did not recall the words spoken by Isaiah the prophet (Isaiah 7:14). Jesus must have found it difficult to believe that every virgin related to King David didn't wake up every day after they reached puberty, thinking, "Today could be the day that I become the mother of the King Whose throne will endure forever."

He must have thought it odd that even though the prophecy had been passed down since the time of David and she had heard it all her life, the thought was incredulous to her. He remembers hearing the indecision in her heart. Nevertheless, Mary agreed (Luke 1:38–44). She called herself the Father's servant and continued to display the heart of a servant as she went to Elizabeth, who was very old and pregnant. She believed Gabriel in her heart. Little did she know that her thoughtful gesture to her aged cousin Elizabeth would provide confirmation of what Gabriel had proclaimed. As soon as she walked into Elizabeth's house, Elizabeth told her that she knew that she indeed was pregnant with the child of God the Almighty (Luke 1:42–43). I'm sure Mary was overjoyed that God had shared the news with at least one other human being.

Admittedly, she agreed to the pregnancy purely by faith and without the understanding that Jesus had. *Poor Mary,* He recalls thinking at the time. If only she knew what it was like in the heavenly realm where the Father's will is always done and everything is always good and perfect. When Father God's will is followed, the consequences are always good. Good always follows His Dad's plans.

He knows that Dad's plans are sure, and they work out perfectly and completely for the good of all. He has watched Dad's plans play out since- well, FOREVER. No one in heaven would be judging her for being pregnant before she actually married Joseph. The entire heavenly population was already calling her blessed for being chosen. The heavenly citizens had been waiting for the implantation of the son of God.

Jesus realizes…This fallen state is all Mary has ever known. The natural limitations of this world are all she is aware of. She does not realize speech is a means of creation. Adam lost this power when he lost the power to dominate the earth and all that is in it. Consequently, man's ability to command unseen things into physical matter greatly decreased. It remained only as imagination. Imagination became the prelude only to what man could create with his hands.

Mary was aware that the Holy Spirit could come upon special people to enable them to perform tasks for God, but that hadn't happened for hundreds of years. Mary knew the Holy Spirit had never come upon her to make her a prophetess or judge over God's people. She was just a young village maiden, living in her father's house, engaged to Joseph, but not yet married. He remembers smiling down lovingly at her. He noticed her humility, her kindness, and compassion and He must have thought, "She's going to be a great mommy." Putting on human flesh must have looked like a pretty good deal if she was going to be the one taking care of Him. And He knew he had kept confidence that Satan couldn't touch Him because He was His Father's Boy. He felt secure (Psalm 22).

Now He is experiencing a reality that to Him is incredulous: His Dad is not there! He is not answering Him as He has always answered every man since man's origin. Jesus knows in His heart that His Father will deliver Him from this horror. He reminds His Father of His origins as a spirit clothed in a human body and given a human soul. They were together then as they've always been. "You, My God, were there when I became a man. It's me, the one who you yourself pulled from Mary's womb…" (Psalm 22:9). Jesus slips back into a reverie as He takes another agonizing breath, hanging exposed and shamed on the Roman cross. He remembers His glorious birth. Hidden from the eyes of everyone on purpose, with only the animals watching as God His Father, was the midwife. Even Mary's husband was not allowed in their presence because according to the law, Joseph would be unclean if he helped; and Father being holy, righteous, and keeping the letter of the law perfectly could not allow Joseph to become unclean by delivering Jesus. Joseph would then have been excluded from the Holy Child's presence.

Joseph

Jesus, who is God and was always with God, knew Joseph's thoughts, as did the Father (Psalm 139:2). Joseph was chosen over all others to be the man who would teach Him the ways of manhood. Joseph possessed a very important quality of character. He was sensitive to the voice of Father God. Just as all human children, Jesus would learn from the example set by His earthly dad. He did not possess any superhuman powers or intellect to manage this world.

He had to experience life on earth just like other people in order to fulfill the requirement to understand our temptations and be a merciful high priest before Father God. According to Luke 2:40 and 52, Jesus would have to grow in wisdom and favor with God and man. In order to maintain the integrity of His sinless nature before God and men, Jesus would have to be raised by a man who also loved, worshiped, and obeyed the Father. Joseph was sensitive to the Father's voice, and he was willing to do whatever he was told, even at the risk of being humiliated and shamed himself. When Joseph discovered Mary was pregnant, he wanted no part of the shame that would surround their marriage. He knew *he* had kept himself prudent before the marriage, but who would believe *that?* He figured the best thing to do would be to divorce her and send her away to prevent shame on him and death by stoning for Mary.

Father decided that an angel would speak to Joseph to explain how Mary became pregnant. The angel came in a dream and explained that Mary was pregnant by the Holy Spirit (Matthew 1:18–21). Jesus remembers how quickly Joseph's faith matured. He obeyed God, ready to endure the anticipation of the gossip among the men in the village that he had managed to seduce Mary before the wedding. He knew there would be coarse joking to endure, and he was innocent. If he defended himself, Mary would be stoned. Instead, Joseph was willing to withstand the shaking heads that would label him as a selfish, undisciplined man, who couldn't wait to have Mary at the proper time, but defiled her before the wedding and produced a baby.

Father God Is the Midwife (Psalm 22:9)

God the Father preserved Joseph's honor and Mary's honor and did not allow shame to be associated with the birth of Christ.

The villagers saw evidence of Mary's pregnancy, but they weren't able to pin down the actual month that Mary gave birth to Jesus. Mary and Joseph were out of town, paying taxes in Bethlehem when Jesus was born (Luke 2:3–7). Thus the prophecy was fulfilled as well.

God adheres to His own laws and Word, above all, therefore, He provided a way for Joseph to remain clean and not participate in the birthing process. This enabled Joseph to worship the Holy Child at His birth. If Joseph had delivered Jesus, he would have become ceremonially unclean and would not have been allowed near the God-child. I can just see Joseph sweating bullets as Mary's labor began and no midwife in sight. If he was like me, he was thinking, "A man's got to do what a man's got to do and I'll just have to repent later, but I'm going to have to get this baby out of Mary myself." God always provides a way to prevent us from committing sin contrary to what His Word requires if we will only trust Him (1 Corinthians 10:13).

There, with gentle hands, God Almighty drew Him gently out of Mary's womb and placed Him at her breast to be nurtured and loved (Psalm 22). Can you just imagine how wonderful that must have felt—God, the Creator, the one who knows how to make everything feel good and look good and taste good prepares your birthing room! He holds Jesus in just the perfect way; His touch is full of love and joy. The lighting is perfect, the entire atmosphere is charged and filled with the presence of Almighty God, and Jesus is surrounded by great joy and held in the arms of love (1 John 4:8)…for the Word of God says that in His presence there is fullness of joy! (Psalm 16:11). His Father spoke, and Jesus' path of life began gently.

Immanuel–God Lives His Life With Us

Jesus was confident that His spoken path would be a virtuous one. His path on earth would be pleasing to His Dad as He stepped into His purpose to destroy the works of the devil and to redeem the world from the evil one (1 John 3:8). Jesus sees His life flash before Him as most men do when the end of this earthly life is near. He has had a happy life. He was accepted and favored by His community from childhood (Luke 2:52). At twelve years old, He spoke in the temple, and the grown-ups were amazed at His wisdom and insight into the scriptures (Luke 2:46–47). He remembers the day John reluctantly baptized Him. It was before Jesus made His public debut. The heavens opened, and God himself spoke so that all could hear. He declared that Jesus was His beloved son.

After that introduction, Jesus walked into His destiny with confidence. Why, everybody heard it. Right in the middle of the Jordan River, God Almighty let everybody know that He was His son (Mark 1:9–11). He came straight from heaven to the womb of Mary. Who could doubt it? It was the greatest day of His life. He must have been walking on air just as we are when we feel great knowing that we are loved by our Father God, when we know we are the apple of God's eye. We are confident that we are walking in the perfect will of God. He started His ministry with an audible endorsement from God and performed a miracle that turned into wine for a wedding celebration. This practically guaranteed a following (John 2:1-11). Yes, life as a man who was also the son of God was actually pretty good. He wasn't thinking about death. Death was the enemy of man! Death was the enemy He had conquered when death thought Lazarus was its prize for four days (John 11:32– 44). Yes, He had conquered death when other men died, and He had to believe that as the son of God, He would conquer death for all of the sons of men.

Above all, all He wanted to do was to please His Father! That is all He has thought about since His arrival from heaven. He had never allowed His mind to think about what was happening now to him now. He recalls that night when the angels announced that He had been born and a whole multitude of angels worshipped and declared Him Lord even though He was in the tiny body of a human. He remembered His Dad let everyone who would look up at the sky know that He had arrived on earth…to be a savior (Luke 2:9–16).

During the time He was with His disciples, He told them that He would suffer and be killed, but that He would be glorified after three days. Once again His Father confirmed His divinity with an audible voice (John 12:23–28). As He told them, He contemplated the ordeal of the cross. He reminded His friends how awful this payment for sin would be. He told them He would suffer and be killed. He explained that He would be going back to His Father because He was not of this world (John 8:23, Matthew 16:21, John 8:21, John 13:31–36). He knew His Father was going to strike Him hard—sin would destroy him, and He would be afflicted, bruised.

He had done absolutely nothing to be chastised for, yet He would suffer the chastisement for all. Isaiah had spoken that He would take the punishment for all of the gruesome, despicable sins committed by those the Father sought to redeem from a fate of their own choosing (Isaiah 53). He would not just be punished for those unspeakable acts of murder and mistreatment of the weak—even children—the perverse sexual sins, the deceit, and robbery; but by faith, He was also going to feel the guilt, shame, and evil of having committed such deeds even though He never performed any sin. By faith, He was going to experience everything the guilty experienced. He would feel the self-hatred and vile shame of it all. For centuries, Jesus had observed how painful it was to endure the suffering that human beings deserved for their unbridled wickedness. He had seen evil and anguish tear at men's souls He had seen sickness and disease destroy their flesh. He felt compassion and cried for them. Then He healed them.

Now it is time to be the savior. He didn't realize that it would be like this. He knew sin's punishment would be an unimagined horror, but He had only seen it from afar! He cries out with anguish unable to comprehend how He has traveled so far from that wondrous day when the angels proclaimed peace on earth, the day of His birth.

In every way, He lived as an ordinary human. His life was governed by the physical and spiritual laws that He Himself established during the foundations of the earth. He confined himself to these laws because they were good (1 Timothy 3:16–17). Notice the spiritual law of the inward witness being confirmed by another and the physical law of two witnesses. The presence of His conception was confirmed to Mary's inward witness by Elizabeth who was also the first physical witness with Joseph being the second.

Simeon and Anna were also two physical witnesses to Jesus' circumcision (Luke 2:21–39). As Andrew Wommack a prominent, current day, Bible teacher points our in His Living Commentary, Simeon also attests to the prominence of the mother in regard to his prophecy of the life of the infant. He does not prophesy to Joseph, Simeon delivers the prophesy to Mary instead of giving it to the father as was the usual Jewish custom (Luke 2:34). Thus amplifying that the seed of a woman (there is no human male seed in Jesus—a man full of the Holy Spirit) will crush the head of Satan and further proclaimin God as the Father of Jesus and Mary a virgin (Genesis 3:15).

At last, the time had come to begin the fulfillment of the assignment He had been given. It had begun. Jesus is not allowed to use divine power as the Son of God. He must live on earth as a human man devoid and empty of any divine and supernatural power. Jesus must function as a human man. Ultimately, Jesus would deal with Satan on Satan's turf as a man! He was the Redeemer of all mankind. Jesus, using wisdom, prepared His spirit. He denied His mortal flesh to strengthen His spirit. He understood, as we must understand, that the battle with Satan is spiritual and requires spiritual muscles (Ephesians 6:12). He fasted (Matthew 4:2).

Satan's goal was—and still is—to make man think that God is not being honest with him. His favorite MO is to place the seed of doubt concerning what God has said about the relationship between himself and Jesus. God had just declared in an audible voice from heaven, 'This is my beloved Son in whom I am well pleased, listen to Him.' (Matthew 3:17, Luke 3:22). So, what does Satan do? He sees that Jesus is hungry. Knowing that hunger is a strong desire of the flesh, Satan presents the satisfaction of hunger as a challenge to the integrity of what God has said to and about Jesus. God said, 'You, Jesus, are my beloved Son.' Satan knows that only a human man can participate in the covenant between God and Man. He knows that Jesus is flesh and blood, a mere human, so, as Jesus is experiencing the human condition of hunger, Satan seizes what he thinks is a grand opportunity.

Satan surmises, that if Jesus is able to interact with him and challenge his authority over the earth, He has to be human, and therefore, Satan believes, "I can use doubt as a tool to cause the man to question who God has said He is and what God said about Him. Above all, Satan wants the man, Jesus to doubt how God feels about Him. He attacks the relationship. Father has told Jesus He is pleased with Him. The underlying message that the devil sends to us and to Jesus is, "Are you sure God is really pleased with you? If God is so pleased with you, prove that He will satisfy your hunger by allowing you to turn these stones into bread." He challenges us, "If God really loves you, why hasn't that... or Why did this...? What Satan does not know is that this human man is filled with the Holy Spirit and walks in the blessing without measure.

Jesus demonstrates how we stop Satan from initiating doubt about who God says we are and how much He loves us regardless of the circumstances. Jesus demonstrates the comeback answer." Man cannot live by bread alone but by every word that comes from the mouth of God." In other words, Jesus shows us that we are to silence Satan with the words that our Father speaks about us and we must believe that the Father loves us as His Word, the Bible, says He does

Hanging from the cross, now, Jesus has no appetite at all. The pain of the nails is too great.

The pain of the nails is too great. He remembers the pangs of hunger He felt out in the wilderness. He had never felt anything like that before. It felt like His stomach was gnawing at the back of itself. He could recall every smell from His mother's kitchen out in the middle of nowhere. Now, having a human body, God identified with the insanity of Esau selling his birthright for some stew and the desperateness of the Israelites eating their children when food was cut off from their cities by enemies. (Genesis 25:29–33, 2 Kings 6:25–29)

A sense of satisfaction pervades Jesus' wearied soul, and He looks ahead knowing that mankind will never be cursed with hunger again at the completion of His mission because He will take on all curses (including hunger) Mankind will be blessed with everlasting provision if they dare to believe in what the Father has promised. This provision includes the third-world countries whose God is the Lord Jesus. Ministries that I support tell of the miracles happening in those countries.

Some people in my church supported a child who became born again and his father asked that we stop sending to his son and help the other children in the village. The 'people' in my church were the children. The children would opt to send the change they received for memorizing Bible verses to the boy, Costa. I was shocked. Our congregation is small and the children are a small group also, but God multiplied what these children sent and abundance came to Costa's home. He is no longer hungry and he wears the best of clothing. He also attends school so that his children (his seed) will prosper.

The Word of God works everywhere there is faith to believe it. The challenge to the relationship with God is for us to believe that God will satisfy our needs when it appears that we will not have our needs met. Turning rocks into bread would not have been a sin, but performing the act as a demonstration to prove that He was the Son of God would have been a sin. More importantly, Jesus did not step in and make provision for Himself. Throughout His ministry, Jesus kept repeating "I do only what the Father tells me to do." His father did not tell Him to make bread for himself from stones. So, He didn't. Unlike most of us including faithful Abraham, who provided Ishmael as his heir instead of waiting,

Jesus waited for God to end His fast. He was completely obedient and dependent on God the Father. Doubting what God says *about* you and *to* you *is`* a sin. . God has said you are His. He is your provider, helper, and deliverer in the time of trouble. If we will focus on our relationship with Him, everything else will be provided.

Out in the wilderness, Satan tempted Jesus by offering power and material wealth. Many times, material wealth can be obtained by doing things that are not according to God's standards. Sometimes, it is quick money to sell something illegal and harmful on the street or go along with something in a large corporate deal. The temptation may come in the form of just not being completely honest or using an inferior material. Cheating on a document, under - or overreporting money may be the temptation.

Sometimes, we form alliances with unsavory people to be successful or popular with the thought that "I'm not going to do what they do." But do you know that God's word says that the company you keep will corrupt you? (1 Corinthians 15:33). "The people I form alliances with or hang around can corrupt me" should be the next thing you say in your heart when you know the character of someone is questionable. Repeating this, you can walk away. Then remember the verse "My God shall supply all my needs according to His riches in glory, in Christ Jesus" (Philippians 4:19), and trust God to promote your career and give you favor in the eyes of man. I have done that many times. It really does work to your advantage to be beyond reproach.

Jesus was tempted to boastfully show off His power to command angels in pride. This too was resisted. We all have been given special talents and abilities, but they are given to us to enhance the lives of others not as a platform for us to be worshiped because we possess these abilities. Jesus never used His powers as God to display what He could do. He only used the power of God flowing through Him as a human empowered by God to help others. Satan is still using the same tactics today. Satan is shrewd. He did not try to kill Jesus because as with the first Adam, Satan did not have the power to kill Jesus. He did have the power to deceive Him and avert His mission. He cannot kill us if we are believers because the Bible says the power of life and death are in our tongues (Proverbs 18:21). And Jesus has stripped Satan of the power to kill us (Revelation

1:18, 1 Corinthians 15:55–57, Matthew 28:18). He can only get us to hurt ourselves by falling prey to his deceptions. All bad things come from Satan, but if we believe what God's word says, we know that we can overcome everything Satan sends our way. Jesus has overcome the world, and we have become joint heirs with Him (John 16:33, Romans 8:17).

Knowing this, Jesus stayed on that cross and went into hell to face Satan and released those godly people who were in Abraham's bosom and ascended back to heaven (Ephesians 4:9–10). When Satan challenges us, we must respond the same way that Jesus did. He used what is available to all of us: the Word of God. What does God's word say? Of course, you have to hear God's Word or read it to have a good comeback (2 Timothy 2:15, 2 Timothy 3:16). During the grueling hours of His sacrifice to redeem us, Jesus thinks about His success in the wilderness adventure and feels another surge of the joy that is before Him. He has demonstrated to the man how to use the Word of God as a sword that will cut Satan like a bandit. He has demonstrated the strategy of overcoming. The strategy is knowing and using the Word of God (Matthew 4:4). He endures because Jesus knows man has been given another means to overcome the deceptive plans of the devil. The mission is on target.

Jesus Knows Trouble is Near (Psalm 22:11)

That night at the Mount of Olives, the reality of it all finally sank in. He knew in a few hours, it would begin. The pain He had witnessed, soon He would feel. Diseased and decaying flesh would replace His smooth skin. Every disease He had made vanish would invade His brain, His heart, His liver. Depravity and psychosis, depression, and hopelessness would come to reside with Him (1 Peter 2:24, Isaiah 53:5). He needed the prayers and strength of His best friends. He needed them to stand in the gap for Him, and they fell asleep (Matthew 26:37-43, Mark 14:33-40). Yes, He knows what it feels like when those you knew would be there just don't have the stamina and fortitude to be what and where you need them to be. They thought they could do it. Just as we feel alone and let down, so did He. Panic raged through Him like a searing hot poker. Fear and the certainty of what was about to happen to Him began to engulf Him to the point that His capillaries burst and blood came through His pores (Luke 22:44).

Satan, who knows the Bible so well, was there to taunt Him. You know how it is. You're living life in this fallen world and Satan brings up a verse in the Bible to us that he twists or takes out of context. Just as it happens with us, Satan was there whispering and hissing out the entire ordeal that Jesus would face. I can just hear Satan reciting His victimization to Him. "You'll bear their griefs and carry all their sorrows that they deserve to carry, and yet they won't even appreciate what you're about to do. None of them will esteem you. Most of the population doesn't even know you exist. They'll all abandon you. Just like they're abandoning you now! Even your so-called "father" will smite you. You will be afflicted and wounded for those useless transgressors. You will be beaten beyond recognition for their iniquities; You will be chastised and they will live forever in peace with your Father, while you will die" (Isaiah 53:3–7). Satan hissed, "You yourself said you were going to die. You have cursed yourself, Jesus! (Luke 9:22) You're mine!" I can imagine Satan delivering the ultimate blow: "Your Father must love those humans more than He loves you. He allows you will be damned so that He can be with them.

Your Father will likely be so happy with the beloved man, that He'll forget all about you. Jehovah never said anything about raising you up on the third day, that is what *You* said. You fool, abort this foolish self-sacrificing fiasco now."

Satan repeated some of Isaiah's prophecies. His goal was to tempt our beloved Savior to abandon us as His friends had abandoned him. Don't think for a moment that Satan didn't display Jesus' future sufferings live and in color. Scenes flashed through His mind like a reel-to-reel movie. I bet the ranch Satan showed Jesus visions of Himself suspended between heaven and earth, the nails in His feet tearing through the skin, tendons, and muscles.

As He rose up to take in air, Jesus remembered every word that Isaiah spoke. He remembered the prediction that He would bear *every* sorrow and experience every iniquity. His throat narrows as it is filled with bile and disgust. He had seen the sorrow of mankind. Sorrow of sickness of the mind, the heart; sorrow from the loss of health; sorrow inflicted by those they love and those they lost. He witnessed the sorrow of being hungry enough to eat one's off spring. The frustration and self-hatred of not being able to break free from an addiction, and seeing inadequacy in the eyes of others. He saw it all, and He had removed a great deal of sorrow since the Holy Spirit gave Him power after His baptism. His father told Him to forgive men and heal them, and He had done just that. That night at the Mount of Olives, He imagined He, Himself, having to experience all of that sorrow, frustration, evil, and pain and He wanted to abort the mission. He had never experienced those emotions. How can you conceive frustration when you have lived perfection? A spoken thought has always become a reality for Jesus. He can't imagine hatred at all. That emotion is not even wasted on Satan and His demons; there is no need. They pose no threat to Him (Luke 10:19). He wanted out. He asked His Father if the beloved man could be redeemed without Him having to go through all of that sorrow evil and pain (Matthew 26:39, Mark 14:36, Luke 22:42).

Deep down in His spirit, He already knew the answer was no. There was no other way. He had done all that He could to restore the health, minds, and reputations of these men and women. He had even raised some souls from the dead temporarily, but the spirit of man remained dead. He had provided their needs, but unless all sin that had been committed or that would ever be committed was blamed on Him and He suffered death as payment for those sins, He would leave the earth and return to His Father and the iniquity, sorrow, grief, sickness, and death would continue to be a part of the human experience forever.

The Holy Spirit would not be able to come to live inside of men if Jesus left them in their sorry state right then. There was another part to this redemption, He had to face Satan and get back the keys of death. He had to face off with him and the demons to get back the earth and dominion of it.

His friends had fallen asleep. They didn't have a clue. His friends had fallen asleep. They didn't have a clue. I'm sure He wondered about these guys as He did about Mary. "Doesn't anybody remember the words of the prophets?" However, He set His resolve to remain faithful to His Father's plan above all; and as always, His Daddy sent angels to comfort Him.

Jesus advances in His tribulation as He has been assured once again that His mission is on track. He thinks, "They are gambling for my clothes. Don't they see they are fulfilling the prophecy?" Jesus is grateful for this reassurance, and He stiffens His resolve to stay the course that His Father has prepared. The plan is unfolding just as the Father said it would. He hopes His closest friends and mother can see that this is God's plan and He is in control. He knows it in His heart, and He rejoices inwardly.

Pangs of loneliness and isolation invade His soul and emotions, however. He trusts His Dad. He knows that He will deliver Him (Matthew 27:43). "Help me!" He continually cries throughout the day and night

(Psalm 22). He cries for help from His Daddy who has always been with Him. They had been together since before the world was begun (John 1:1–2). He had bragged to everyone "I and the Father are one" (John 10:30). "I am in the Father and the Father is in me" (John 10:38).

He was mocked and teased about the apparent lack of the Father's presence while He hung on that Roman cross of crucifixion. He remembers how He himself had declared that all the miracles that He performed were done by God through Him. Jesus boldly told them, "My Father sent me and He is working through me" (John 8:42). So now they look at Him and they laugh and say, "If He was from God and He had such a great relationship with God, why hasn't God delivered Him from this cross?" (Mark 15:27–32, Psalm 22). He looks through the centuries past, and He revisits the many times men were not worthy of His Father's deliverance because they were disobedient, but they trusted Him and He delivered them always (Psalm 22).

He reminds His Father that He is a loving and merciful God. "Father," He laments, "You answered them always! Time after time, You answered them, even when they despised and turned away from you. I remember their hearts were filled with anger towards You and You still rescued them! They counted on You and they were never disappointed" (Psalm 22) (Begin new paragraph) "But me, I am nothing to You. I am calling for help and I am but a lowly worm crawling on my belly. You ignore me. They who have gotten Your favor are watching me suffer." (Psalm 22). He was stripped of His clothing, without dignity, and laid for the whole world to gawk at as if He deserved to be shamed. But in reality, He never sinned He had done nothing to bring disrespect upon Himself. Yet the very ones who committed the disgrace of killing an innocent man and setting a murderer free, had thefavor and forgiveness of God Almighty (Matthew 27:14). Jesus imitated His Father in this also. He uttered, "Forgive them because they don't understand what they are doing." (Luke 23:34).

He had never been separated from His Father. He knew what sin looked like, but He had never felt it. The shame and disgrace of it made Him feel despair, but the loneliness of sin was daunting. He was fully aware that His Father was no longer with Him. Only after Jesus fulfilled the atonement for our sins could God promise never to leave us. Jesus could not claim that promise. God was not with Him. He was left utterly and entirely alone with all of the wickedness and evil and suffering and sickness ever created or endured since Adam sinned. Six thousand years of sin became His (Psalm 22). "Not my will, but your will," He repeats, silently hanging between heaven and earth. He forces His mind away from the motion picture that recounts the treachery of man. Instead, He thinks of those waiting for His mission to be successfully completed. All the people of every nation including members of His earthly family that are in Abraham's bosom are watching, waiting for Him to pay the vow of salvation (Luke 16:22, Psalm 22:25).

I can see Satan at the crucifixion during those crucial hours when Jesus is becoming sin and our iniquities and diseases are entering Him on the cross. Satan whispers to the Messiah, "You're dying, you will never see any of these people so precious to You ever again. You are going to be in hell with me. All this suffering is for nothing. You can't even save yourself." One of the criminals Jesus hangs between agrees with Satan (Luke 23:33–39; Psalm 22).

Jesus' resolve is renewed as He remembers His earthly father, Joseph, and the tender times they spent together in the carpenter's shed. He reminisces about the patience and kindness in Joseph's voice as he taught Him how to create smooth and beautiful furniture from a tree. He can still feel Joseph's large rough and calloused hands over His small smooth ones as they move together along the grain of the wood. His love for His earthly daddy fills the corners of His mind that Satan's words cannot reach. "Only I can remove the reproach from Joseph and his relatives." He breathes, "King David had Urias killed because he made Urias's wife pregnant. Rahab was a prostitute. Why the very household in which I lived carried multiple stigmas of iniquity that were forgiven but not yet paid for. That payment requires the sinless blood of God," He thinks, and the joy of knowing that He and the Father will live with them all again gives Him joy for the present trial. They, we, all of humanity, needed His blood. He was being poured out too, just as the Psalm said (Psalm 22:14).

Although the Father is silent, the following conversation gives testimony of the miracles that the Father has performed through Jesus and speaks loud and clear magnifying His innocence and deity. This conversation confirms that men have been paying attention and believing the good news that He indeed is Lord and Savior. One of the criminals rebukes the other. He tells him that they both deserve this punishment, but Jesus has done nothing wrong. Then as if the Father is using this doomed man to remind Jesus of His own royalty and the grace that His death will bestow upon the guilty and condemned criminal, the thief says to Jesus, "Lord, remember me when You come into Your kingdom." As always, Satan is exposed as a liar. This unworthy criminal knows who Jesus is and believes that this is not the end of Him. "He turns to the criminal who knows he is unworthy, and Jesus assures the man that he will live with Him in paradise—that day." Don't miss this demonstration of Jesus' purpose on the earth. A perfect demonstration of God's grace and our faith is captured in the small intimate exchange between Jesus and the criminal. The criminal knows he is guilty and must suffer the consequences by man's hands but he comes boldly to his Savior and asks to be remembered because he recognizes that He is royalty of a kingdom more glorious than those of man. Although he knows he is guilty and undeserving, response? He does not falter or size him up or even ask if he is sorry for the wrong he has done. Jesus answers him with confidence . Don't miss it. this day…the day that the unworthy, guilty criminal asks Jesus to remember him, is the day that his request is granted. (Mark 11:24).

There is no chance for confession, no possibility for the criminal to get it right. All he has is the heart to believe that Jesus can remember him, unworthy as he is (Romans 10:10, John 11:26, John 3:16–17, Hebrews 11:6, Romans 2:4). In this exchange, the devil is shown to be a liar—men do remember who Jesus is, and they are appreciative and they believe in Him. This small exchange reminds Jesus of the joy before Him (Hebrews 2:2). Jesus knows that today, He will die as the criminal, and His new disciple will be in Paradise—Abraham's bosom, where Jesus will enter triumphantly and set the righteous captives free that have been awaiting His arrival. The criminal who acknowledges Jesus as the savior will be set free to live in heaven with those who have died in faith. Jesus thinks about all of the hope that has produced the faith that has covered the centuries of sin. Hope in the redemption of all mankind (John 8:56). Hope in the man that will be born from above. The hope of a new man that will not only know God's Word and strive to fulfill it but the man that will carry the Spirit of God inside of him.

In Psalm 32, David speaks about the blessed state of the man who will have a spirit that is without deceit. He is speaking of our born-again spirits. The spirit that is completely righteous. This could only refer to the spirit of God that replaces our dead spirits when we pass from death to life. Jesus recalls that Jeremiah the prophet has said that mankind "will know intuitively right from wrong because God has put His laws in their hearts" (Jeremiah 31:33). Jesus believes that He will be raised from death and be the first to be reborn by believing the Word of God that was spoken. He had spoken His faith and said that after three days He would rise again. (Mark 8:31) Just as those words believed by Jesus achieved His rebirth, the Word of God works the same miracle for each man who believes in his heart and makes an outward confession with his mouth that he or she believes that Jesus gave His life so that we might have the blessing of Abraham, be God's friend, reconciled to Him forever with the new covenant (Romans chapter 5).

The miracle takes place when you believe. Even the desire to tell what has happened to you is effortless. You can't help yourself. After Jesus was raised from the dead, other men inherited the capacity to be reborn of the Spirit of God (Colossians 1:18). The Word of God is a seed that germinates and produces the new you, which will be born of the Spirit from above. Just as four thousand years of God's Word produced Jesus, when we hear the good news of God becoming a man to redeem us and believe it, we are "produced" as He was, from above. "As He is, so are we, in this world" (1 John 4:17). All the blessing without works—that is what Abraham, David, and all the others hoped for in the promise of being made new. What they hoped for, we can experience (Galatians 3:14).

They could not experience the rebirth themselves because they had already gone to Abraham's bosom before Jesus came to established the new covenant by fulfilling the old one (Matthew 5:17). Now hanging on the cross, Jesus thinks, "Mankind will truly be like God once again as I am," (1 John 4:17). Jesus chose to focus on what His three days of suffering would accomplish (Romans 5:11–21). He recites His purpose in His heart. "I will take the punishment for their sins even before they commit them. My payment will stand for generations that have not been born yet, just as Adam's sin stood to curse men that weren't born yet." (Romans 6:10, Hebrews 10:12–14). "Every man that believes that I have taken the sin from them will experience a new birth. They will be a new creature, born from the spirit of God who is in heaven above" (2 Corinthians 5:17). "Man has always been a spirit being, but that spirit has been dead since Adam sinned. I am the first man that will die a physical and spiritual death and be reborn with the spirit of God" (Colossians 1:18). "The sin that I am now absorbing will cause spiritual death in me as it has for men all these years. When I have defeated Satan and taken the keys to death, hell and the grave, I will be raised from the dead by the Holy Spirit" (Romans 8:11, Revelation 1:18).

As He endures the beatings, the ravages of diseases, and the crucifixion, in His mind, He evokes images of His reward. "At the completion of my mission, I will have sisters and brothers whose spirits are alive to God. Now a new spirit straight from the Father will be born inside of

"Now a new spirit straight from the Father will be born inside of each believer's body, just as I am now of my Father's Spirit, which is in a body. They can commune with me and the Father as Adam did before the sin. That Spirit will be undefiled by sin, holy and perfect as I am perfect, always in perfect harmony with the will of the Father. Each man will know when he has received the newborn Spirit in his heart. He will hear the Word of God that will explain to him what has taken place by my crucifixion, death and resurrection. When that man hears the truth, which is an incorruptible seed, that truth will germinate in his heart and the rebirth will occur. He will know that he has been born of the spirit and he will know that he is a child of the most high" (Romans 8:16)

The rebirth is explained in the Bible in the book of Romans, Chapter 8, verses 5 through 16.I must interject to tell you about my personal rebirth. I didn't even know what the term "born again" meant. I had heard it, but I attributed it to some weird was of living. I put those people in the same category with the hippies and the Black Panther Party, the skinheads, and everyone else who had what I called an alternative lifestyle…unusual from mainstream America. They believed something I considered divergent. I didn't know what it was. I wasn't judging. I just didn't know. I am living proof that there is no particular feeling, but there is a sense deep inside that something has changed and the change brings relief (Romans 8:9-:11). An invisible weight is lifted. Your mind becomes conscious of a new way to look at things. I began to do things that were straight out of the Bible without knowing that they were in there.

I started singing and dancing to the Lord when I woke up. I used to consult my horoscope every morning and for some reason, it just popped into my head…"I wonder what God thinks about that?" I had no idea that it was wrong. Everybody I knew who professed to be a Christian read their horoscope daily. As I went about my usual tasks, I sat down at the top of my staircase to do something. I think I was putting on my socks. I laid my Bible down (I was rushing out of the house and taking it with me). Bam! Just as I dropped the Bible onto the step, it opened to the story about Saul consulting a witch about his future (1 Samuel 28:7). Then I heard the biblical story about the king who consulted a false prophet about his illness, and God sent word by the true prophet that the king would die because he asked the false prophet about his future instead of asking God if he would get well (2 Kings 1:16).

What I know is when you believe the story about God coming to earth as a man to remove your sin and make you a part of God's family, you are not the same good person. You are a new person who is driven by God's Spirit to please Him.(Romans 8:6-8) The more you read your Bible and are around the Word being spoken, the more the Spirit within you directs you to live in such a way that love pours out of you. I was going to exact revenge on an administrator who touched me where he shouldn't have and refused to give me a makeup test when I wouldn't let him continue to molest me. I had been hospitalized for a major surgery and missed two weeks of medical school. All through medical school and residency, I had planned to bring this man to public embarrassment and ruin as much as possible. Without any conscious effort or purposeful suppression of my anger, I no longer wanted to exact that revenge. I didn't know about vengeance being the Lord's. In fact, I forgot about wanting to destroy that man until years later.

When I remembered, I no longer felt a desire to see the man suffer for what he had done. I couldn't believe what had happened myself. After planning his downfall for years, I just forgot. I also started hearing God direct me to do things for people. I gave people money without a second thought when I didn't know when I would get more money myself. I just believed that God would take care of me because the Bible said He would supply all my needs. I had never known any Christians who acted as if they really believed what the Bible said, and I didn't know what the Bible said until then, so, I thought that all the Christians that really believed, lived in the abundance of God's provision just as the Bible says. The money I gave to others was *seed*. Giving when you need the money yourself, is the principle of "sowing out of your lack" I had no idea that was a principile that would bring abundance, but it did. This principle is taught in 1 Kings 17:10-15. The word of God contains spiritual principles and laws that work even if you are not aware of them. Just like gravity.

You don't have to drop something it falls to the ground. In the same way, there is an assurance that a change has come in you and you don't have to do anything to bring it about except hear the Word of God and believe it. That Word will change you. I don't care how busy you are. I was raising two children as a single parent and starting a solo medical practice with no collateral when I became a born-again Christian. I didn't have time to spend hours in the Bible, but I had a hunger and a desire to know what God thought about me and my life. The new Spirit knows what to do Himself once He comes to live inside of you.

The Mission Continues Jesus didn't expect this horrible loneliness of being separated from the one who had always been a part of Him. Even when He took on a human body, He knew Dad was there. He told people, "I and the Father are one" (John 10:30). Now He experienced the heart-wrenching feeling of being utterly alone and distanced from His Father, who is part of His being. loneliness engulfs Hin and overwhelms Him, filling His soul with the darkness and shame inherent and inescapable, because sin's envelope has it all.

Betrayal by Judas, He understood. Now Now, He looks into the betraying eyes of Peter. Even though He had told Peter that Satan would test his loyalty and that he would fail, it still hurt. It hurts Him the way it hurts a loyal wife who knows her husband is gone to sleep with another, and she still waits for him to eat the meal she has lovingly prepared, or the businessman who knows his employee whom he has trusted is stealing. It hurt Him because we hurt. He had to feel all of our sorrows and be tempted. He was tempted to hate and not to love the people who were hurting Him. He was betrayed and abandoned by most of the people who claimed to love Him, and those who did stay at the foot of the cross stood by watching, too frightened and shocked by His apparent powerlessness to utter one word in His defense. What could possibly be said or done? He had been the One— the One filled with power, the Deliverer, the Messiah.

There He was, dumb like a sheep about to be sheared (Isaiah 53:7). And then there is silence from His Father God. Silence is all there is now. There are no angels sent this time. He has become a sin. He is headed for hell.

Jesus was in a mess, and He was calling for help. You know what that feels like. It's when you're at that place on the road of life after that wrong turn. Sometimes, it is a sinking feeling immediately after the deed. Most often, that feeling comes with the consequence of the secret decision that seemed so innocent but landed us at that place. You're in a mess… and you feel overwhelmed by circumstances and you feel that God is far away. The sin has encased you and made you feel alone and ashamed. You imagine not even God is there. And for Jesus, He wasn't. Ah! Alas, there is a difference here. Jesus did not take any wrong turns. Remember? He grew in wisdom. He made all of the right decisions, which should lead Him to what is conducive to happiness and prosperity. He has done only what His Father told Him to do.

We, you, me—all of us—have not regarded the Lord our God with such esteem. We have made poor choices and have taken the wrong road. Yet Jesus can remember His Daddy rescuing everybody else from their wrong choices. His Dad was patient with His other children. God would watch broken heartedly as they did evil for years, and then He would deliver them…no matter how much they deserved to be left to suffer the bondage they created through disobedience. He always caused the fallen, disobedient, hardheaded humans to triumph. Jesus screams for His Daddy to deliver Him, but to Him, His Father and His God is silent (Psalm 22).

The breaking of the law brought wrath (Romans 4:15, Ephesians 2:3), but now, because He sacrificed Jesus and emptied His wrath on Him, for you and for me, God the Father is there, no matter what ! (Romans 3:24–25).You may feel like God is not there because you are guilty; in your heart, you know that you haven't done what you were supposed to do. You are at fault. This isn't your first rodeo, but it is the first time you've been caught. He is there, and He loves you anyway and when you look back at the wrong turn, you'll see that somehow God changed the road and you ended up in a good place with blessings in spite of your mistake. Yes, He really does work all things out so that they turn out good for those who love Him and fulfill the purpose for which they were born (Romans 8:28). I have seen this happen in my life, not just many times, but every time.

If you believe that Jesus was sacrificed so that you can be forgiven for your sins, God isn't ever going to be upset with you again. Your agreement with God is under the New Covenant and remember, that covenant has no requirements. It is unconditional, like the rainbow covenant. You just have to believe it. He will always rescue you and never be angry with you (Isaiah 54:9). You are treated just like Abraham was treated before Moses was given the law. He still loves you and will rescue you. The consequences of your actions may be inflicted by man and society, but your Father, God will not. You are in the family and your big brother Jesus took the rap. He suffered the consequences that you deserved. Because you are His Father's child, God promised to work everything that happens to your good. (Romans 8:28). He is with you and so are ministering angels. The angels are there to minister to you. If you pay attention, you will see them at work on your behalf. Favor will be granted above what you deserve. You will know that He is with you even in your reaping of the evil you have sown. Why? Because you are His child, and He gave you His word. He promised to always cause you to triumph. (2 Corinthians 2:14). He promised to never be angry with you again. If you believe that Jesus was sacrificed, He is there; and even though you made a bad decision, He isn't upset with you. He still loves you and will rescue you. He said, "I will not hold their sins against them or be angry with them ever again." He won't turn His back on you, ever, no matter how you feel or what sin you commit because God turned His back on the one child from His own DNA. He turned a deaf ear to the one who had been so totally obedient to His every desire. He turned His back!"

It took one man, Adam, who It took one man to take His wrath away and make us all righteous, restoring everything back to the way it was intended to be (Romans 5:12).

As I said before, dominion was given to the man. The man gave the dominion to Lucifer, who then became Satan and was allowed to kill steal, and destroy…using the power given to him by man. Only a man could fulfill the covenant and redeem what was given away. Only a man who could totally withstand the temptations of Satan could be victorious, so the Father spoke a man into a human womb. The man with God's own blood flowing through Him, Jesus. That is the reason Christians believe that belief in Jesus is the only way to avoid the consequences of sin and separation from the Creator forever.

Suspended between heaven and earth, Jesus remembers what He gave up to redeem mankind. He can't forget the glory He left behind in heaven. The love, joy, and total peace and security of His Father's presence. He visualizes the splendor of the unbridled beauty of heaven's colors, the gold streets, the precious stones, and pearls—all given up because His Father wants to spend eternity with the man, and He does too. He sets His resolve! He thinks about being one with the man again. There will be humans that are completely holy… forever without them having to do anything…This eerie separation from His Father must take place so that the man may have all that He has. The man will once again be allowed to bask in the glory of the heavenly place. The man will once again be lord over the earth and be citizens of heaven if they choose it. They will have complete access and ownership to the marvels of heaven and the desires of their hearts on earth. The man will again create wealth with his own mouth; sickness and addictions sewn into the fabric of life on earth by Satan will be commanded away (Colossians 1:12–14). It has all been decided; He says, I will give my all, I will become(this is the same discourse by Jesus

It has all been decided; He says, "I will give my all, I will become completely emptied, the man will inherit the riches of heaven. Dominion over the riches of the earth will once again belong to those who believe in the miracle of my task. Dominion over principalities, powers, and everything that has a name will be given to the men who decide to have faith to believe in my Father's promise. The fullness of time has come" (Ephesians 1:20–Ephesians 2:1). (New Paragraph Jesus is not speaking now)

He had never felt it—sin and the horrible feelings that abide inherently in sin had never been a part of His experience (2 Corinthians 5:21). This whole ordeal had been painful. His earthy friend betrayed Him, but He knew that was going to happen. The wisdom that His Father had filled Him with over the years gave Him great discernment regarding the character of people He encountered on earth (James 1:5). He knew what was in the heart of Judas (John 13:27). He knew the limits of Peter's commitment beforehand (Matthew 26:34). He had seen individual humans experience betrayal and He saw their disappointment, and He was prepared for that. He had experienced disappointment while growing up. But never has His Dad not been there. He entered this earthly realm with the assurance that Satan couldn't defeat Him. His Dad has always been His God (Psalm 22). He had supplied all His needs; whenever there was trouble, Dad was there. He functioned as a human, but as the human with the assurance of God's power, the assurance that He knew His prayers were answered every time.

He remembers all the miracles that He performed on behalf of man. Lazarus coming alive after being dead with decaying flesh restored… He cries out and reminds His Dad, "You were there then, you answered me" (John 11:41–42). "You moved me from the presence of the mob that threatened to throw me over a cliff. I didn't even have to call out to you, you just allowed me to walk right through their midst" (Luke 4:28–30). "You warned Joseph to take me away to Egypt when the babies were slaughtered" (Matthew 2:13). You have always protected me. Where are you? I AM IN TROUBLE NOW, THE WORST YET, AND I NEED YOU TO DELIVER ME NOW!" He had to have faith that even now, He would ultimately *win!* How it must have torn at the very core of His soul to remember all the times when His Father answered the prayers and calls from the hateful, disobedient human man. Father has always answered the man who willfully turned his back on all of the goodness that He and His Father had together provided for the man Adam in the garden. Eve was deceived by the devil, but still, Adam *gave* it away.

Jesus had watched mankind perform centuries of willful defiance, and time after time, His Father showed mercy and answered them even in their disobedience. Where was that mercy now? He calls out to His father, and everyone hears, "Why have you forsaken me?" (Psalm 22). And then He stops. He does not let the crowd hear the rest of His seemingly futile cries to His Father. He does not allow the crowd around Him to further humiliate Him by basking in His Father's obvious betrayal of the unfailing trust in God that Jesus has always displayed. Jesus has been like Abraham, Daniel, David and all the others who found His Father the Almighty God faithful to deliver them in their hour of need. He, like all the others, knew His Father to be faithful to deliver Him, and He has boldly proclaimed that His Father would even send angels to rescue Him (Matthew 26:53)… but…this time, He was not going to be delivered; there would be no rescue. Since He was tempted at all points as we are tempted (Hebrews 4:15). He was tempted with the sin of self-righteousness. He was tempted to say, "Look, Dad, I have never done anything vile, but they have done it all." And we have, but He took all of the punishment on Himself in our place (1 John 2:2). Father God has heard and answered when the descendants of Jacob called Him. Jesus reminds His Father, "You came to their rescue even though they continue to scorn your ways and your Word. They sing of the mighty exploits that you have performed on their behalf. They should have nothing but praise for the way you have always rescued them. They know they haven't deserved Your faithfulness, so they praise You, and yet, they fall back into their sinful ways. They even destroy themselves, and You have mercy and restore them." In this way, Jesus experienced the temptation to doubt that God cares and the temptation to accuse God of not rewarding His faithfulness and obedience (Psalm 22). He could have reminded His father, "I moved when you said move. Why, we move as one. Remember, I told them you and I are in each other?" (John 10:30, John 14:11–13). I'm sure that Satan was right there to remind Jesus of what a good and faithful son He had been. The prophetic Psalm 22 captures the pitiful cries of the betrayed Son to His Father; however, to those present at the crucifixion, His pathetic outcries are inaudible.

The apparent betrayal is obscured from the gloating onlookers as He is engulfed by hell's torments those three days. Only those who remember Psalm 22 would be privy to Jesus' relentless cries to His Father for rescue. Even in His suffering, He chose to keep the agony of the perceived betrayal between the two of them. He loves His Dad and wants to think the best of Him. He has to have faith that He will be glorified as He glorifies His Father (John 17:1, John 17:4–5) despite what He experiences, for He knows His Father cannot lie. Those three days started on a Wednesday, not Friday. He spent three whole days in the bowels of hell, just as He had told His disciples (Mark 8:31). The Bible says that the mysteries of God are hidden but revealed to those who are sons. The crucifixion took place on the High Sabbath, which is on Wednesday, not Friday. In grief, He measures the vast distance that sin has placed between Himself and His beloved Father and asks, "How is it that you are now so far from me?" (Psalm 22). He knows the answer: the sin has placed the gulf between what is holy and what is vile. The Father is Holy. He cannot interface with sin without consuming it in fire. The burnt offerings were consumed in man's place, allowing the human race to survive until Jesus Himself could become that lamb sacrificed as a burnt offering. Jesus knew three days would be spent in hell's fire. In faith, He has released His Spirit to take on death.

The Second Phase of His Mission

Jesus is there now. He is enveloped by the presence of evil and depravity.

He is enveloped by the presence of evil and depravity. Unbearable pain from every disease imaginable has ravaged His human body so that it does not appear human (Isaiah 52:14). Jesus has borne every negative emotion and now, fear, the essence of them all, is heightened. As He spirals down into hell (Ephesians 4:9), He describes bulls that are not ordinary, but bulls of Basham. Basham bulls fed on very fertile grasslands and were therefore huge. He has breached the demonic realm. I believe He is describing demons that are magnified; they are humongous and terrifying demons. The demons in hell have manifested themselves to appear as fierce, strong, giant, powerful long-horned bulls that are closing in on Him and torturing Him. The mighty demonic bulls are stomping their powerful hooved feet as they surround Him. They snort out a foul, scorching, hot breath. They march and stomp around the wretched man, Jesus, exhibiting a confident ability to overwhelm Him. Him. They demonstrate the power to annihilate Him. The twenty-second psalm says "He called out loudly, but His Father. The twenty-second psalm says He called out loudly, but His Father did not hear Him.

With Jesus, the hope of glory confined to his territory; Satan assembled his army of demons. They are the evil spirits that are the perpetrators of every evil deed committed by men the world over. Neither demons nor Satan himself can perform in the realm of the earth without flesh to cover them. A man with a body has to obediently perform the evil deed. They are the spirits that moved the hands to pierce Jesus' hands and feet (Psalm 22:16).

This is the same spirit that collaborated with Judas to betray Jesus. High priests were commanded not to tear their clothes even at the death of their children (Leviticus 21:10, Leviticus 10:1–6). This is the spirit that provoked the high priest to sinfully tear his clothes and accuse Jesus of blasphemy (Matthew 26:65). These are the gamblers that won the cloak He was wearing when He was arrested (Psalm 22:18, John 19:24). These are the hands that drove the crown of thorns into His brow. These are the mouths that told twisted lies at the mock trial and expelled spit into His face. Here in gleeful attendance is the one who drove a sword through Him. The gawking, gloating, onlookers that tell Him to save Himself. The demons that shouted to have Barabbas released are chanting their victory now. Sitting smug and satisfied is the demon who turned on Judas, convincing him to hang himself when Jesus was dying to forgive him. They are the spirit of all injustice, murder, deceit, and theft. Gathered here are the perpetrators of every evil that has ever been committed by anyone, and they are also the cause of every pain and sickness suffered. These depraved spirits close in on Him. Satan has summoned them all. Encircling like a pack of mad rabid dogs foaming at the mouth, they move in for the ultimate kill (Psalm 22). The devastation of hope for God's man has finally been accomplished. Jesus transitioned from life to death (Revelation 1:18). He gave up His life, on purpose (Matthew 27:50, Mark 15:57, Luke 23:46, John 19:30).

When Satan tossed His shredded, lifeless body into the pit of fire, that evil creature was satisfied that he would be free to bring the very existence of hell to the earth. Man would be eternally separated from God because the Savior was dead. The Savior's body was dead, His soul was dead. And because He had become sin, by the Word of the Lord God, His spirit was dead. The Hope of humanity's redemption and glory was dead and defeated—burning in the eternal flames forever! The savior had become sin, and the Father could not commune with sin, so "two for the price of one." Satan surmises happily, "The man's redeemer, gone, and without redemption, man would never again be the ruler of the earthly realm." Satan recalls all the scripture that condemns man and he is certain that the condemnation of Jesus is complete. His demise is iron-clad, sewn up, and tied by the Word of the Lord God Himself! sin! The gateway to hell has become the man Jesus and the man Jesus is sin! And the wages of sin is death! Satan howls a spine-tingling, evil laugh.

God Is a Consuming Fire (Hebrews 12:29)

Satan remembers the Father is Holy. He cannot interface with sin without consuming it in fire.

I guess Satan forgot that God had also said in Psalm 16:10 that He would not leave Jesus in hell, and His body would not see decay. Jesus is and always was God—and yes, God is a consuming fire Himself, so it was that when Jesus's dead spirit hit the fire, it was ignited by the power of the Holy Spirit; and instead of burning up, His incorruptible Spirit grew and consumed all of the sin. Sin burnt off Jesus like chaff and dross burned to reveal pure gold. The fire of the Holy Spirit spread through His entire being, filling Him with new life. He was a pure and holy Spirit once again. Just as King Nebuchadnezzar saw an extra person in the furnace, Satan saw something extraordinary in the blazing pit (Daniel 3:24–30). Jesus was not being consumed, but He was consuming the fire and gaining strength from it. His purified Spirit was becoming more and more powerful, with each blazing flicker of each tongue of fire. Thus Christ emerged from hell's fire alive with the Spirit of God and stripped Satan of all the power he had held over mankind.

After defeating Satan in hell, Jesus moved into Sheol, Abraham's Bosom, where the spirits of those who had died believing in the promise of righteousness through the Messiah were awaiting the fulfillment of the promise. Those who had died in faith left the resting place of Abraham's Bosom and rejoined their bodies. So much was the life-giving power of Jesus that these previously dead people were seen walking about the earth (Matthew 27:52), resurrected by the power of the Spirit of the living God (Romans 8:11). Death could no longer hold anyone who believed in the redemption and atonement performed by Jesus (1 Corinthians 15:55).

Jesus was setting the captives free (Ephesians 4:4– 9). Satan's power was stripped. The curse was reversed because Jesus was a man, and He had kept the law perfectly. Just as Adam's choice to disobey and bring the curse on all men, Jesus' perfect obedience now reversed the curse for all men (Romans 5:12, 1 Corinthians 15:21). Death could not hold Him because He was righteous. He had earned no wages of death, but His blood had been poured out. He, as the sacrificed lamb, had died and the burnt offerings were performed.

Atonement had been made. It was finished. Jesus was heard asking only that those being used by Satan and his demons be forgiven (Luke 23:24). He does not ask for forgiveness although He carried the heavy sins. He asked to be delivered from the torture, the pain, the ridicule. He knew He had to bear the sin for He has willfully exchanged His righteousness for the sins of every man (2 Corinthians 5:21). Because He suffered abandonment, the Father is free to remove the curses and embrace us.

This time, when the curses were removed and placed on the lamb sacrifice, it counted forever. For the lamb was God's own Son, and because it is a known medical fact that the blood of a child comes from His Father, the sacred blood of God Almighty runs through the veins of Jesus (Hebrews 9:11–12, Hebrews 10:10). When He was raised from the dead, perhaps He ascended to heaven and He sprinkled His own blood on the true mercy seat in heaven like the one that was reproduced in the earthly temple (Leviticus 16:14-16). The Bible does not tell us what Jesus did when He ascended into heaven. This is what the Bible says in John 20:11-17. Mary was crying outside His empty tomb. She thought Jesus had been stolen. He stopped to let her know that He had not been stolen but had been raised from the dead. He would not let her touch Him, and He said "Don't touch me. I have not yet ascended to my Father." Then in Hebrews 9:12, Paul says Jesus, as our High Priest, entered the Most Holy Place with His own blood and once and for all obtained eternal redemption. Only Jesus could have said, "But me, I have been a faithful obedient son. I haven't done any of those things. I have courageously proclaimed all that you have given me to say. I have done all that You have told me to do, and I have done everything exactly as you told me to do it." He obeyed the law of God completely, and He gave it all away to you and me. He removed all the credit from His account. He emptied it—and gave it to you.

At the completion of His glorious mission, the whole world rejoices. The families of every nation now worship the Lord God Almighty because the veil of the Most Holy place was torn from heaven downward. (Matthew 27:51) When Jesus gave up His life on the cross, the veil to the Holy of Holies in the temple at Jerusalem was literally ripped in half. God did this to demonstrate the removal of a barrier between man and Himself. Now may enter into His presence with thanksgiving and boldness (Hebrews 10:19-20). We have been reconciled. Every nation, wealthy and poor, can now worship and bow before the King of kings and Lord of lords. God the Father has given Jesus reign over all things in heaven and earth. The twenty-second psalm says that generations that have not been born yet will know about redemption. Everyone will benefit from the redemption brought by the blood of Jesus. This is the Good News, the Gospel.

What was lost to Satan by Adam has been redeemed and given back to mankind Jesus was. given all power, and as a man, He has all authority to work God's plans for the kingdom through the lives of those who believe. Jesus is righteous, and He has imparted righteousness to each believer. You are born from death in sin to life in Christ. You share an inheritance with Christ, which is far above anything you can imagine. He does exceedingly above what we can ask or think, according to the power that works within us. That means that we have the power inside us to speak to situations and things. We have to make the power work according to the will of God. We know the will of God by what the Bible says is His desire for us. Jesus died and rose and ascended over two thousand years ago, and we are still praising Him and benefiting from His sacrifice. Dominion over everything that has a name has been given to Him, and He has given that power to us. Without Him, we are unrighteous and powerless. With Him, we are righteous and full of power. He has left the Holy Spirit that dwells inside every believer. We are never without God's power if we believe He is who He says He is. Jesus has made us joint heirs to all things pertaining to life and godliness. He took on the shame, the sorrow, the pain and suffering, and the blame for every sin because He wanted us to have the power of the Holy Spirit and to know Him and His Father intimately, without limits. Every desire we have is met when we take time to know God through His word (1 Peter 1:3). He positioned you and me in a precious place, above all that He had in heaven, above His life and comfort and all this world had to offer… **He thought of us above all** and took the fall so that we could have all that was lost to Satan in the garden. This is love—not that we loved God, but that He loved us and sent his Son as the atoning sacrifice for our sins (1 John 4:10).

Milton Keynes UK
Ingram Content Group UK Ltd.
UKHW050255071224
451734UK00003BA/20